I0017674

AI UNMASKED

Is humanity ready for what's coming?

Are we prepared for a world where ai makes the decisions?

Jaxon Cole P.

Copyright © 2025 Jaxon Cole P. All Rights Reserved.

No part of this book may be reproduced, stored in a retrieval system, or transmitted in any form or by any means, electronic, mechanical, photocopying, recording, or otherwise, without prior written permission of the publisher, except for the use of brief quotations in a review.

Table of contents

INTRODUCTION

Artificial Intelligence AI. It's a phrase that has been buzzing around for years, but only now is it beginning to demand our attention. Once confined to the pages of science fiction, AI is rapidly reshaping the world around us. From the moment you unlock your phone with a fingerprint to the algorithms curating your social media feed, AI is no longer something of the distant future. It is here, and it is evolving at a pace that leaves us both in awe and, at times, uneasy.

In the last decade, we've seen AI go from a niche concept to a revolutionary force. What started as simple automation in industries has blossomed into complex systems capable of learning, thinking, and even creating. We now have AI that can write poetry, drive cars, diagnose diseases, and offer advice—tasks once thought to require distinctly human intelligence. What's even more remarkable is that this evolution is just the beginning. Every day, AI's influence deepens, and its role in our lives grows ever more central.

But here's the question that demands our attention: Is humanity truly prepared for AI's increasing ability to make decisions that impact our lives? While we've embraced AI in certain areas, we haven't fully grappled with the extent to which it will shape our future. As AI grows more capable, its decisions will extend beyond simple tasks it will influence critical areas like healthcare, law, business, and even our personal interactions. The implications of this shift are enormous, and the truth is, we may not be ready for all that lies ahead.

In this book, we'll explore the profound ways AI is already affecting various sectors. From the doctors relying on AI to make diagnoses, to businesses using AI for personalized marketing, and even the ways AI is helping solve global challenges like climate change, it's clear that this technology is already integrated into the fabric of our daily lives. But we must also ask, what happens when AI doesn't just assist us, but makes decisions for us? What kind of world will we be living in when AI is at the helm?

This book invites you to join me on a journey to understand the power and potential of Artificial Intelligence. We'll explore its vast impact, its benefits, and its risks. And ultimately, we'll confront the question that looms over it all: Are we, as a society, ready for the world AI is creating?

CHAPTER 1

Understanding Artificial Intelligence

Artificial Intelligence (AI) is not a futuristic concept, it's the present reality, quietly reshaping the world as we know it. But what exactly is AI, and why does it matter? At its core, AI refers to the technology designed to enable machines to simulate human intelligence. It's not about creating human-like robots, but rather about building systems that can learn, reason, and make decisions in ways that resemble human cognitive abilities.

AI's primary role is to replicate functions that humans typically perform with their intelligence. It achieves this through complex algorithms and vast amounts of data. Unlike traditional machines that follow a set of predefined instructions, AI systems are designed to "learn" from data, making them adaptable and capable of improving over time. This unique quality of AI gives it an edge in tasks where human intelligence, with its complexity and nuance, is often required.

Fundamental Capabilities of AI

Learning At the heart of AI lies the concept of learning. Like humans, AI systems are designed to learn from

6

experiences. However, rather than relying on trial and error or traditional schooling, AI learns by processing large datasets and recognizing patterns within them. The more data AI systems process, the better they can understand and predict outcomes. Machine learning, a subset of AI, refers to this ability—where algorithms improve and evolve based on the data they encounter.

Problem-Solving One of the hallmarks of human intelligence is our ability to solve problems, whether simple or complex. AI mirrors this by analyzing problems and developing strategies to reach solutions. Unlike humans, AI can process vast amounts of data at speeds far beyond our capabilities, allowing it to solve problems more efficiently. Whether it's diagnosing a disease, predicting stock market trends, or recommending the next movie, AI's problem-solving abilities have profound implications in nearly every field.

Decision-Making AI doesn't just process information—it makes decisions. Once it has learned and analyzed data, it can draw conclusions and take action. These decisions range from simple—like filtering your email inbox for spam—to life-changing, such as determining the best course of action for a patient's treatment plan. AI decision-making isn't random; it's based on patterns and probabilities derived from data, often making it more accurate than human decisions in specific contexts.

Comprehension Beyond learning and decision-making, AI also strives for comprehension. While it may not "understand" the world the way humans do, it can process and interpret information in ways that allow it to provide meaningful insights. From understanding spoken language to interpreting images and videos, AI's ability to comprehend the world around it has made significant strides. Technologies like Natural Language Processing (NLP) allow AI to grasp the nuances of human communication, making interactions more intuitive, whether through voice assistants or customer service bots.

AI's Expanding Role

The most impressive aspect of AI isn't just its ability to mimic human thought, but its potential to surpass it. AI systems aren't confined to the tasks they were initially programmed for. As they process more data and refine their algorithms, they continually improve and take on more complex roles. Today, AI is playing a crucial role in fields like healthcare, where it can diagnose diseases with incredible accuracy, and in finance, where it predicts market fluctuations.

Yet, as AI becomes more capable, we must ask ourselves: How far can it go? Can AI truly replicate the depth of human intelligence, or is it merely a tool for amplifying our own capabilities?

In the next chapters, we'll delve deeper into AI's applications and explore the future possibilities and potential risks that come with it. But first, it's essential to understand that AI is more than just technology—it's a reflection of how far we can push the boundaries of what machines can do, and perhaps, even what it means to be intelligent.

In the world of Artificial Intelligence, machine learning and deep learning stand as the powerful engines driving its rapid advancements. While AI itself is about enabling machines to perform tasks traditionally requiring human intelligence, it is machine learning and deep learning that allow AI systems to evolve, improve, and function autonomously.

Machine Learning: Teaching Machines to Learn

At its core, machine learning (ML) is the process by which machines "learn" from data. Instead of being explicitly programmed to carry out specific tasks, ML algorithms are designed to identify patterns in large datasets and make predictions or decisions based on that data. It's similar to how we humans learn from experience: we analyze past situations, recognize patterns, and apply that knowledge to new challenges.

For example, a machine learning model trained on thousands of images of cats and dogs can learn to recognize which images contain which animal. Over time, as it processes more data, the model becomes increasingly accurate at distinguishing between the two. This is the foundation of many AI applications we encounter daily— from recommendation engines on Netflix and Amazon to facial recognition software.

There are two main types of machine learning:

1. Supervised Learning: In supervised learning, the model is provided with both input data and the correct output. It then learns by comparing its predictions to the actual answers, adjusting its algorithms to minimize errors. This approach is used in applications like email spam filters and fraud detection in banking.

2. Unsupervised Learning: In unsupervised learning, the model is given input data without labeled outcomes. The goal here is for the model to find

hidden patterns and relationships within the data, such as grouping similar customers based on purchasing behavior. This type of learning is essential for tasks like clustering and anomaly detection.

Deep Learning: The Brain Behind the Brain

Deep learning is a specialized subset of machine learning that takes things a step further. It mimics the way the human brain processes information using a structure called neural networks. These networks consist of layers of interconnected nodes—just like neurons in the brain—that work together to process and learn from data.

What sets deep learning apart from regular machine learning is its ability to handle vast amounts of unstructured data—things like images, sounds, and text. A deep neural network, with its many layers of nodes, can sift through millions of pieces of data, identifying complex patterns and making highly accurate predictions.

For example, deep learning algorithms are behind technologies like self-driving cars, which must analyze video footage from sensors and cameras to make decisions in real-time. Similarly, deep learning powers speech recognition in virtual assistants like Siri and Alexa, enabling them to understand and respond to natural language with impressive accuracy.

The Backbone of Modern AI

Together, machine learning and deep learning are the backbone of modern AI. These technologies enable AI systems to learn from experience, adapt to new information, and make decisions that were once thought to be uniquely human. In fact, many of the groundbreaking advancements we've seen in AI, such as real-time language translation, medical image analysis, and autonomous vehicles, are the direct result of these techniques.

The ability to continually learn and improve without human intervention makes machine learning and deep learning incredibly powerful tools. As AI continues to evolve, the boundaries of what's possible with these technologies will expand, bringing us closer to a future where machines are capable of understanding and performing tasks that are fundamentally human.

Artificial Intelligence, once a speculative and futuristic concept, has evolved into an indispensable part of our modern world. Over the past few decades, we've witnessed AI's journey from its infancy in narrow applications to the ambitious pursuit of Artificial General Intelligence (AGI), a vision that, while still unfulfilled, could potentially change the course of human history.

From Narrow AI to Artificial General Intelligence (AGI)

The AI we interact with daily is known as narrow AI or weak AI. Narrow AI is designed to perform specific tasks—such as facial recognition or playing chess—better and faster than humans, but it lacks the ability to handle broader, more complex activities. For example, a machine learning model used to recognize objects in images is excellent at its task, but it can't apply that knowledge to new areas like language translation or strategic decision-making without significant reprogramming.

In contrast, Artificial General Intelligence (AGI) represents a future vision of AI that can understand, learn, and apply intelligence across a wide variety of tasks, just like humans do. AGI would not be restricted to specific, pre-defined functions; it could solve complex, unforeseen problems in any domain—be it science, technology, or even human emotions.

While AGI remains a goal, it is still largely theoretical. We are still in the era of narrow AI, but the progress we've made in this area has laid the foundation for what could eventually lead to AGI. For now, AI systems are incredibly powerful within their narrow confines, but their capabilities do not extend beyond the tasks they are specifically designed for.

AI Applications Already in Use

AI is already a significant part of our lives, often working in the background without us even realizing it. Here are a few examples of AI applications that have seamlessly integrated into modern life:

1. Speech Recognition

AI-powered speech recognition systems, such as Apple's Siri, Amazon's Alexa, and Google Assistant, have revolutionized the way we interact with technology. These systems use natural language processing (NLP) and machine learning to understand and respond to spoken commands. From setting reminders and sending messages to controlling smart home devices, speech recognition AI is transforming how we manage tasks throughout the day.

2. Image Recognition

AI has made leaps in image recognition, which allows machines to analyze and interpret visual data. Platforms like Google Photos use AI to automatically organize and tag photos based on their content, recognizing faces, landmarks, and even animals. In healthcare, AI is helping radiologists by analyzing medical images for signs of diseases such as cancer, often with accuracy comparable to or exceeding that of human doctors.

3. Recommendation Systems

Have you ever found yourself binge-watching a new show on Netflix or shopping for products on Amazon based on suggestions? That's AI at work. Recommendation systems use AI algorithms to analyze your preferences, behavior, and historical data to suggest products, movies, music, or even news articles. These systems have become integral to our online experiences, shaping everything from what we buy to how we entertain ourselves.

4. Self-Driving Cars

The field of autonomous vehicles is one of the most exciting applications of AI. Companies like Tesla, Waymo, and others are developing self-driving cars that use AI to process data from sensors and cameras, enabling the vehicle to navigate roads, avoid obstacles, and make decisions in real-time. AI's role in self-driving cars is a complex one, as it combines deep learning, computer vision, and reinforcement learning to safely and efficiently operate a vehicle.

AI in Our Lives Without Us Noticing It

While these applications are noticeable, many of AI's contributions are far more subtle. We often interact with AI without even realizing it. When you use a GPS system to find your way, you're relying on AI's ability to analyze traffic patterns and suggest the fastest route. When you shop online, AI is quietly at work, recommending items based on your browsing history and preferences. Social media platforms use AI to curate your feed, showing you posts that align with your interests.

Even in areas like banking, AI is already playing a critical role. Fraud detection systems monitor transactions in real-time, looking for patterns that indicate unusual or fraudulent activity. Similarly, in the background, AI is helping companies optimize their supply chains, ensuring that products are available when and where they're needed. These applications have become so integrated into daily life that we often take them for granted.

In fact, AI is woven into the fabric of so many industries that its influence is often invisible. The next time you unlock your phone, interact with a virtual assistant, or receive a movie recommendation, remember: AI is already shaping your experience, even if you don't always see it.

CHAPTER 2

The Mechanics of AI

How Does AI Work?

At the heart of every AI system lies an intricate and powerful process that enables machines to learn, adapt, and make decisions—processes that allow AI to solve complex problems, make predictions, and even understand the world in ways that resemble human thinking. But how exactly does AI accomplish all this? It comes down to a combination of algorithms, vast amounts of data, and a method known as training.

Algorithms: The Brain of AI Systems

The first piece of the puzzle is the algorithm. An algorithm is essentially a set of rules or instructions that tell a machine how to approach a task. In the case of AI, algorithms are designed to process data, recognize patterns, and make decisions. These rules aren't static or pre-programmed like those in traditional software; rather, they evolve as the system interacts with new data, allowing the AI to improve its performance over time.

For example, consider a self-driving car. The algorithm it uses must decide how to navigate the road, detect obstacles, and respond to changes in traffic conditions. These algorithms are built on complex mathematical models and are continually refined as the system gains more experience.

Data: The Fuel for AI

Data is what powers AI. Without data, AI systems would have nothing to learn from or make decisions about. Think of data as the raw material that an AI system uses to train itself, much like a student using textbooks to study for an exam. The more diverse and extensive the data, the more capable the AI becomes.

AI systems rely on vast datasets that can come in many forms—numbers, text, images, sound, video, and more. These datasets feed the AI models, enabling them to discern important patterns and relationships within the information. For example, a machine learning model trained on thousands of images of dogs and cats can learn to distinguish between the two animals by analyzing thousands of visual features such as shape, color, and texture.

But it's not just about volume quality matters too. The data must be accurate, representative, and relevant for the specific task the AI is trying to learn. Garbage in, garbage out, as the saying goes. If the data is biased or incomplete, the AI's predictions and decisions can be flawed.

Training: The Learning Process

Once AI has access to data, the next crucial step is training. Training involves feeding large amounts of data into the system, allowing the algorithm to "learn" by identifying patterns and making predictions based on the information it has processed. This phase is akin to teaching a child how to solve problems by providing examples and correcting mistakes along the way.

In supervised learning (one of the most common types of machine learning), the algorithm is given both the input data and the correct output. For instance, in an image recognition task, the AI might be shown thousands of labeled images of cats and dogs and told which is which. Over time, the AI refines its ability to recognize cats and dogs by adjusting its algorithm based on the patterns it identifies in the data.

However, training doesn't always need supervision. In unsupervised learning, the algorithm is provided with data without any labels or predefined answers. Instead, the AI must find its own patterns within the data. For example, unsupervised learning can be used to segment customers into distinct groups based on purchasing behavior, even if we don't tell the AI what categories to look for.

Through repeated exposure to data and continuous adjustments to its internal models, the AI system improves its accuracy. The goal of this training process is for the AI to not only recognize patterns in known data but also make predictions when it encounters new, unseen data.

Pattern Recognition: Spotting Connections in Data

One of AI's most powerful abilities is pattern recognition the capacity to identify meaningful relationships and trends in data. Pattern recognition is what enables an AI system to excel in tasks like image recognition, speech processing, and fraud detection.

For instance, when you use facial recognition software, the AI isn't simply matching a picture with a name. It's analyzing thousands of tiny features like the distance between your eyes or the shape of your jawline and comparing them to patterns it has learned from a database of facial images. Over time, as the system encounters more data, it gets better at identifying subtle patterns, even recognizing faces in different lighting, angles, or environments.

In applications like fraud detection, AI looks for patterns in financial transactions. If a customer typically makes small purchases in a particular area, but then suddenly buys large items from an unfamiliar location, the AI can flag this as an anomaly an early indicator of potential fraud. The more data it processes, the more proficient it becomes at distinguishing between regular behavior and unusual patterns.

Prediction-Making: The Power of Anticipation

Once an AI system has learned to recognize patterns, it can begin making predictions. This is the true power of AI: not just analyzing data, but using that analysis to anticipate what will happen next.

Consider a recommendation system on Netflix or Spotify. After observing your watching or listening history, the AI can predict which movies or songs you are most likely to enjoy next. The system doesn't just pull from a list of random options it uses its understanding of your tastes and patterns to suggest content that aligns with your preferences.

In healthcare, AI can predict a patient's likelihood of developing a condition based on their medical history and lifestyle data. In financial markets, AI can forecast stock movements, helping investors make more informed decisions.

Ultimately, AI's ability to predict outcomes based on past data opens up possibilities in virtually every sector, from optimizing supply chains to improving personalized services.

Machine Learning and Neural Networks

Artificial Intelligence (AI) isn't just about building systems that can think and act autonomously. It's also about creating systems that can learn from experience, just as humans do. At the heart of modern AI lies machine learning (ML), a powerful method of creating intelligent machines by allowing them to learn from data. This approach has transformed how AI systems are built, making them increasingly capable of performing tasks that were once reserved for human intelligence.

The Primary Method for AI Creation: Machine Learning

Machine learning is the process by which AI systems improve their performance over time by learning from data, without explicit programming. Rather than hardcoding specific instructions, we teach the machine to recognize patterns in the data it receives, helping it make decisions or predictions based on those patterns.

For example, in the case of a self-driving car, instead of programming the vehicle to understand every possible scenario on the road, machine learning allows it to learn from vast amounts of data. The car analyzes data from sensors, learns how to identify objects like pedestrians and traffic signs, and uses this knowledge to make real-time driving decisions.

The most significant strength of machine learning lies in its ability to adapt. As AI systems process more data, they can continuously refine their algorithms to enhance their decision-making ability. This ability to improve autonomously makes machine learning incredibly powerful and versatile, applicable to tasks ranging from email filtering to facial recognition.

The Role of Algorithms in Machine Learning

Algorithms are the backbone of machine learning. These are the mathematical procedures or sets of rules that AI systems use to process data and learn from it. Each machine learning algorithm has a unique way of analyzing data and making predictions.

For instance, some machine learning algorithms, like decision trees, make predictions by following a series of logical decisions based on the data they are fed. Others, like support vector machines or k-nearest neighbors, focus on classifying data points into categories based on similarities.

No matter the algorithm, machine learning works through a continuous feedback loop. The AI system applies an algorithm to data, makes a prediction, checks whether that prediction was correct, and then adjusts the algorithm to improve future predictions. The more data it processes, the better the algorithm becomes at making accurate predictions.

Neural Networks: The Brain of AI

When we talk about machine learning and AI, it's impossible to ignore neural networks. These are computational models inspired by the human brain, designed to simulate the way neurons process and transmit information. Neural networks have revolutionized the field of AI by enabling machines to learn from data in a more complex and nuanced way.

A neural network consists of layers of nodes (also known as neurons) that are connected to each other, much like the neurons in our brains. Each node processes a piece of data and passes it on to the next layer. The more layers there are, the deeper the network, which leads to the term deep learning.

These networks are incredibly good at recognizing patterns within data, and that's what makes them so powerful. Neural networks are the reason AI is so good at tasks that require sophisticated pattern recognition—things like image recognition and natural language processing (NLP).

Neural Networks in Action

1. Image Recognition Neural networks, particularly convolutional neural networks (CNNs), are the cornerstone of modern image recognition. These networks can analyze visual data pixel by pixel and identify objects within images. For example, CNNs are used in facial recognition systems that can identify a person in a crowd or the self-driving cars that must recognize pedestrians, cyclists, and other vehicles on the road.

The network "learns" to recognize features in an image, such as edges, colors, and shapes. The more images it processes, the better it becomes at distinguishing subtle differences between objects, making it an indispensable tool in fields like security, healthcare, and entertainment.

2. Language Translation Neural networks also play a significant role in language translation. Systems like Google Translate use deep learning to translate

text between languages. The neural network learns from vast amounts of bilingual text data, analyzing sentence structures and grammar rules across different languages. Over time, the system gets better at understanding context, idioms, and nuances, allowing it to produce translations that are more accurate and natural.

3. Natural Language Processing (NLP) Natural Language Processing (NLP) is another area where neural networks shine. NLP enables machines to understand and generate human language. Whether it's chatbots answering questions, voice assistants transcribing speech, or AI systems analyzing customer reviews, neural networks are the foundation of these applications. They break down human language into manageable pieces, identifying syntax, sentiment, and context, and use that understanding to generate meaningful responses or actions.

Deep Learning: Expanding Neural Networks

When we refer to deep learning, we are talking about neural networks with many layers—often dozens or even hundreds of layers—capable of handling extremely complex tasks. Deep learning models can learn to recognize more intricate patterns in data, such as the emotional tone in a piece of text or the subtle differences between two nearly identical objects in an image.

For instance, deep learning allows voice assistants like Siri or Alexa to understand complex commands with varying accents or noisy environments. It also enables AI to generate realistic art, compose music, or even create new video game levels.

CHAPTER 3

Types of AI

Weak AI vs. Strong AI

As Artificial Intelligence continues to advance, it's essential to understand the difference between Weak AI (often called Narrow AI) and Strong AI, which represents a future vision of what AI could potentially become. These two concepts highlight the varying levels of intelligence and capabilities within the field of AI, ranging from highly specialized applications to a more generalized, human-like intelligence. Let's take a closer look at each of these types of AI.

Weak AI (Narrow AI): Mastering Specific Tasks

Weak AI, also known as Narrow AI, refers to AI systems that are designed to perform a specific task or set of tasks. Unlike humans, these systems are not capable of generalizing their intelligence across different areas or adapting to new, unforeseen situations. Instead, Weak AI excels in solving problems within a limited domain and is highly efficient at automating particular processes.

For example, voice assistants like Siri or Alexa can respond to specific queries, set reminders, and control smart home devices. However, they are not capable of doing anything outside of their programmed scope. They can't, for instance, switch from helping you cook dinner to conducting scientific research or engage in meaningful conversations about philosophy.

Other examples of Weak AI include:

- Recommendation engines on platforms like Netflix or Amazon, which suggest movies or products based on past behavior.

- Facial recognition systems used for security or social media tagging, where AI identifies and labels people's faces in photos.

- Self-driving cars, which use AI to recognize road signs, avoid obstacles, and navigate streets, all within a specific and highly controlled set of driving conditions.

Weak AI is incredibly powerful within its narrow scope, but it remains limited in that it cannot go beyond the tasks it was specifically designed to perform. It's not truly "intelligent" in the human sense because it lacks general problem-solving skills, emotional understanding, and creativity that humans possess. For now, nearly all AI systems fall under the category of Weak AI, and they are primarily used to automate specific tasks to save time and improve efficiency.

Strong AI (Artificial General Intelligence - AGI): The Vision of Human-Like Intelligence

On the other end of the spectrum lies Strong AI, also known as Artificial General Intelligence (AGI). Strong AI refers to machines that can understand, learn, and perform any intellectual task that a human being can. Unlike Weak AI, AGI would not be confined to a specific domain; it would possess generalized intelligence, capable of solving problems, learning new things, and adapting to various tasks without the need for human intervention or pre-programmed instructions.

In theory, AGI would be able to perform complex tasks that require creativity, emotional intelligence, and critical thinking, just like humans. It could engage in abstract thinking, draw conclusions from limited data, and even develop original ideas and innovations. For example, an AGI could analyze global economic patterns, predict the outcomes of geopolitical conflicts, and write a novel—all in a way that closely mimics human thinking.

Some potential capabilities of AGI include:

- Creative Problem-Solving: Unlike Weak AI, which is limited by predefined rules, AGI would be capable of solving problems in a variety of fields, including scientific research, healthcare, and the arts, in ways that are not pre-programmed.

- Transfer Learning: AGI could apply its knowledge from one field to another, something that current AI systems cannot do. For instance, it could transfer knowledge from playing chess to strategic military simulations or medical diagnostics.

- Human-like Understanding and Empathy: AGI could potentially understand human emotions, reason through ethical dilemmas, and develop deep social understanding, allowing it to interact with people in meaningful ways.

- Autonomous Self-Improvement: An AGI system could learn and improve on its own without human supervision, a significant leap beyond Weak AI, which requires data and human input to enhance its performance.

However, despite the promise of AGI, it is still a hypothetical concept. No system today possesses true general intelligence, and building an AGI would require significant breakthroughs in how we understand cognition, learning, and consciousness. Some experts believe that AGI could emerge within the next few decades, while others argue that it may be centuries before such technology is feasible—or that it may never exist at all.

The Potential Future of AGI

The pursuit of AGI is one of the most exciting and controversial topics in the field of AI. The capabilities of AGI are difficult to predict with certainty, as they would depend on our ability to replicate human-like intelligence in machines. However, many experts believe that AGI could transform nearly every aspect of society, from solving complex global issues like climate change to revolutionizing industries such as medicine, law, and education.

While AGI promises vast potential, it also raises significant ethical and existential concerns. If machines could think and act like humans, would they deserve rights? Could they surpass human intelligence, and if so, what would that mean for the future of humanity? These questions are at the forefront of AI research, and the development of AGI would require careful consideration of the risks and benefits.

As we continue to advance in AI, it is important to recognize the distinction between Weak AI, which is revolutionizing industries today, and the long-term possibility of AGI, which could challenge our very understanding of intelligence and autonomy.

The Four Levels of AI

As AI technology continues to evolve, it's essential to understand the different stages or levels of AI that have been proposed. These levels help to categorize AI based on its capabilities, ranging from simple systems that respond to their environment to more complex and speculative forms of intelligence that may one day exhibit human-like awareness. Let's explore each of these four levels of AI.

1. Reactive Machines: Responding to the Environment

The most basic form of AI is Reactive Machines. These are AI systems that can respond to specific stimuli or input from the environment but lack the ability to store memory or use past experiences to inform their decision-making. In essence, reactive machines can only react to what they are currently experiencing, and they cannot use historical data to improve or adapt.

A classic example of a reactive machine is IBM's Deep Blue, the chess-playing computer that famously defeated world chess champion Garry Kasparov in 1997. Deep Blue's AI was capable of evaluating millions of possible moves in a game of chess and responding accordingly, but it did so without any memory of past games or the ability to learn from previous matches. It had a predefined set of rules for evaluating board positions and making moves, and that's all it could do.

Reactive machines are incredibly useful for tasks that don't require decision-making based on historical context. They excel in environments where responses need to be fast and precise but where context and learning are less important. While they are highly efficient within their domain, they are not adaptable to new, unforeseen situations outside of their programming.

2. Limited Memory AI: Using Past Data to Make Predictions

Limited Memory AI represents a more advanced level of AI, capable of storing and using past data to inform current decisions. Unlike reactive machines, limited memory systems have the ability to access and process historical information, allowing them to make predictions and adapt their responses based on what has happened before.

A key example of limited memory AI is ChatGPT, the AI language model you're interacting with right now. ChatGPT processes large amounts of conversational data and uses that historical information to generate contextually relevant responses. In other words, it remembers the conversation within a single session, adjusting its answers based on previous interactions.

Self-driving cars also rely heavily on limited memory AI. These vehicles collect data from their environment, including information about road conditions, traffic, and pedestrians, and store that data to inform real-time decision-making. For instance, a self-driving car will use its historical data to adjust its route based on patterns it has learned, such as traffic patterns or typical obstacles along certain streets. By drawing from past experiences, limited memory systems can improve their efficiency and make more accurate predictions.

Limited memory AI represents a significant step forward in terms of adaptability. While it doesn't have long-term memory or the ability to learn beyond its training, it's capable of responding intelligently to changing environments based on past data.

3. Theory of Mind AI: Understanding Human Emotions (Not Yet Realized)

Theory of Mind AI takes a huge leap beyond limited memory AI by introducing the idea of systems that can understand and interpret human emotions. This level of AI is based on the concept that machines could eventually understand human feelings, intentions, beliefs, and desires, and use this understanding to make better decisions and interact more naturally with people.

The term "Theory of Mind" refers to the psychological concept that humans have an understanding of other people's mental states—such as emotions, thoughts, and intentions—and can predict and react based on that understanding. For AI to possess a theory of mind, it would need to not only recognize human emotions but also respond in ways that are appropriate and empathetic.

While this level of AI is still in the realm of science fiction, researchers are making strides toward developing machines that can detect emotions through facial expressions, voice tone, and body language. For example, some AI systems are already capable of analyzing facial expressions to gauge a person's emotional state. However, these systems don't truly understand emotions in the way humans do; they simply recognize patterns associated with certain feelings.

Theory of Mind AI would represent a breakthrough in human-computer interaction, allowing AI systems to communicate and collaborate with humans on a much deeper, more emotional level. But as of now, this level of AI remains hypothetical, with significant technological and ethical challenges standing in the way.

4. Self-Aware AI: The Future of Conscious Machines (Speculative)

The final level of AI—Self-Aware AI—is the most speculative and, at present, purely theoretical. Self-aware AI would not only be able to understand emotions and make decisions based on context and history but also possess consciousness and self-awareness, much like humans do. This level of AI would have the ability to reflect on its own existence, understand its role in the world, and make independent choices based on its internal state and external environment.

A self-aware AI would likely possess the ability to recognize itself in a mirror, understand its purpose, and potentially even experience emotions or desires. This goes far beyond the scope of current AI technology, which operates based on algorithms and data processing without any sense of self.

The potential implications of self-aware AI are profound. Would a self-aware AI have rights? Could it experience suffering or joy? How would humans interact with an AI that is conscious and potentially capable of making moral and ethical decisions? These questions open up a vast and uncharted territory in the study of AI and consciousness.

At present, self-aware AI exists only in the realm of science fiction, and there are significant philosophical and technical obstacles that would need to be overcome for such a system to be created. But it remains an area of intense interest and debate among AI researchers and ethicists, as its creation could fundamentally alter the relationship between humans and machines.

CHAPTER 4

Why AI is Important

The Growing Influence of AI

Artificial Intelligence is no longer a futuristic concept; it is already deeply woven into the fabric of our everyday lives. The capacity for AI to analyze vast amounts of data, solve complex problems, and automate tasks is changing industries and improving how we work, communicate, and solve some of society's biggest challenges. As AI continues to grow in capability, its influence is becoming increasingly pervasive and transformative.

AI's Ability to Analyze Data, Solve Complex Problems, and Automate Tasks

One of AI's greatest strengths is its ability to process and analyze massive volumes of data far more efficiently than humans can. Today, AI can sift through datasets containing billions of data points, quickly identifying patterns and correlations that might take a human weeks, months, or even years to uncover. This incredible speed and precision allow AI to make data-driven predictions, automate decision-making processes, and even recommend solutions for complex problems.

For example, in the healthcare industry, AI is capable of analyzing thousands of medical records to identify patterns in patient histories, diagnoses, and treatments. With this data, AI can help doctors make more accurate predictions about patient outcomes, enabling earlier interventions and personalized care. AI's ability to continuously learn from new data also ensures that it improves over time, making it a powerful tool for solving increasingly complex medical, financial, and logistical problems.

AI's ability to automate tasks is another key factor in its growing influence. By taking over repetitive, time-consuming jobs, AI frees up human workers to focus on higher-level tasks. In industries like manufacturing, AI-powered robots are performing everything from assembling products to conducting quality control. In offices, AI tools are automating everything from scheduling meetings to analyzing customer feedback, allowing employees to work more efficiently and effectively.

The Benefits of AI in Various Industries

AI's influence spans across various industries, each benefiting from AI's ability to streamline processes, improve decision-making, and enhance efficiency. Below, we explore how AI is transforming three major industries: healthcare, finance, and manufacturing.

Healthcare

AI is revolutionizing the healthcare industry in several ways, primarily through its ability to analyze medical data and improve patient outcomes. AI-driven tools help doctors make quicker and more accurate diagnoses by analyzing medical images, genetic data, and patient records. For example, AI can detect early signs of diseases such as cancer by scanning X-rays and MRIs, identifying anomalies that might be missed by the human eye. These systems are increasingly accurate and can assist healthcare professionals in making faster decisions.

In drug discovery, AI is being used to sift through vast chemical databases to identify promising compounds for new medications. AI is also playing a key role in personalized medicine, where treatments are tailored to an individual's unique genetic makeup. By analyzing data from clinical trials and patient histories, AI can recommend the most effective treatment plans, improving outcomes for patients.

Finance

The finance industry has embraced AI for a wide range of applications, from fraud detection to predictive analytics. AI-powered systems can monitor financial transactions in real-time, analyzing vast amounts of data to detect unusual patterns that may indicate fraudulent activity. By identifying suspicious transactions almost instantly, AI can prevent financial losses and protect consumers from fraud.

In the world of predictive analytics, AI is being used to forecast market trends and evaluate investment opportunities. Algorithms that analyze historical market data can predict future price movements, allowing investors to make more informed decisions. In banking, AI-driven credit scoring models use data from a variety of sources to assess an individual's creditworthiness, improving the accuracy of lending decisions and reducing the risk of defaults.

AI is also transforming customer service in the finance sector, with virtual assistants and chatbots offering real-time support to customers. Whether assisting with balance inquiries or helping clients navigate financial products, AI-powered tools are improving the customer experience and increasing operational efficiency for financial institutions.

Manufacturing

In the manufacturing sector, AI is being used to optimize production processes, reduce downtime, and improve safety. AI-powered robots are used for tasks ranging from assembly to packaging, reducing the need for human labor in potentially hazardous environments. These robots can also be programmed to identify and fix errors in production lines, ensuring that products are manufactured with greater precision and at a faster rate than ever before. Additionally, AI is playing a role in predictive maintenance, where machine learning algorithms analyze sensor data from factory equipment to predict when a machine is likely to fail. By scheduling maintenance before a breakdown occurs, manufacturers can avoid costly downtime and improve the efficiency of their operations.

Examples of AI's Current Contributions

AI is already having a major impact on several key areas of business and society. Here are some of the most notable contributions that AI is making today:

Predictive Analytics

AI's ability to analyze data and make predictions has been particularly transformative in areas like demand forecasting and inventory management. For example, retail companies use AI to predict consumer purchasing trends, allowing them to optimize their stock levels and avoid overstocking or understocking products. Similarly, AI is used to forecast future sales, helping businesses make more accurate financial projections.

Personalized Marketing

AI is revolutionizing the way companies approach marketing by providing highly personalized customer experiences. By analyzing vast amounts of consumer data, AI can segment audiences based on behavior, preferences, and purchase history. This allows businesses to deliver personalized ads, emails, and recommendations tailored to individual customers. AI also optimizes marketing campaigns by predicting which messages will resonate best with different groups of consumers, increasing the effectiveness of marketing strategies.

Fraud Detection

AI has made significant strides in fraud detection, particularly in the financial services industry. AI algorithms can analyze transaction data in real-time, identifying suspicious patterns that might indicate fraudulent behavior. Whether it's detecting unusual credit card activity or spotting anomalies in insurance claims, AI is helping businesses and financial institutions reduce the risk of fraud and financial crimes.

Autonomous Systems

Self-driving cars are perhaps the most well-known example of autonomous systems powered by AI. These vehicles use a combination of AI technologies, including computer vision, machine learning, and real-time data analysis, to navigate the roads without human intervention. Beyond transportation, AI is also being used in other autonomous systems, such as drones for package delivery and warehouse robots for managing inventory, marking a shift toward greater automation across various industries.

AI in Everyday Life

Artificial Intelligence has evolved beyond being a buzzword or a futuristic concept; it has become an integral part of everyday life. From the moment we wake up to when we go to sleep, AI is at work, shaping how we interact with technology and the world around us. You might not even realize it, but many of the everyday technologies you use are powered by AI, making life more convenient, efficient, and personalized.

How AI is Integrated into Common Technologies

Smartphones and Smart Assistants

One of the most ubiquitous ways AI is integrated into our daily lives is through smartphones and smart assistants. These devices use AI to anticipate our needs, answer questions, and make recommendations. Voice-activated assistants like Siri, Google Assistant, and Alexa are powered by AI algorithms that understand natural language, allowing users to interact with their devices hands-free. These AI assistants can do everything from setting reminders and sending messages to playing music and controlling smart home devices. Their ability to understand and respond in real-time makes them indispensable in modern households and workplaces.

AI is also behind many of the features that make smartphones more intuitive, such as predictive text, autocorrect, and facial recognition for security. By continuously learning from user interactions, these systems improve over time, offering more accurate predictions and becoming smarter with each use.

Smartphones are now essential AI-powered devices that have become central to daily life.

Online Recommendation Systems

Another example of AI in everyday life is the online recommendation systems used by platforms like Netflix, Amazon, and YouTube. These services use AI to analyze your past behavior what you've watched, bought, or liked to predict what you might want to do next. The algorithms that power these recommendations constantly learn from your interactions, refining their suggestions to match your evolving preferences.

For example, Netflix's recommendation engine takes into account what movies or shows you've watched, the genres you prefer, and how you rate content, then uses that data to suggest what to watch next. Similarly, Amazon uses AI to recommend products based on your previous purchases and browsing history, making it easier to find things you're likely to be interested in.

These recommendation systems rely on machine learning algorithms to understand patterns in large datasets, providing users with more personalized and relevant content, and enhancing the overall user experience.

The Role of AI in Transforming Industries

AI's influence isn't confined to personal devices; it is also radically transforming entire industries, making operations more efficient, improving services, and creating new opportunities. Let's look at how AI is reshaping industries like healthcare, education, retail, and customer service.

Healthcare

In healthcare, AI is revolutionizing diagnostics, patient care, and medical research. Machine learning algorithms are now able to analyze medical images, like X-rays and MRIs, with a level of accuracy that rivals human doctors. AI systems can identify abnormalities, such as tumors, and assist in making faster, more accurate diagnoses.

Additionally, AI-powered systems are increasingly being used to personalize patient care. By analyzing patient histories, treatment outcomes, and genetic information, AI can help doctors create more individualized treatment plans. This is particularly useful in fields like oncology, where precision medicine is becoming more prominent. AI is also playing a key role in drug discovery, helping researchers identify potential drug candidates faster by analyzing large chemical datasets.

Education

In education, AI is being used to create personalized learning experiences for students. AI-powered tools can assess a student's strengths and weaknesses, then recommend learning materials tailored to their needs. This has the potential to revolutionize how education is delivered, making learning more efficient and accessible.

For example, AI-driven platforms like Duolingo use machine learning to help users learn new languages. These platforms track progress, provide feedback, and adjust difficulty levels based on the learner's pace, creating a customized learning environment. In classrooms, AI tools can assist teachers by grading assignments, tracking student performance, and even offering real-time insights into areas where students may need additional help.

Retail

AI is transforming the retail sector by enabling businesses to offer more personalized experiences for customers. AI-powered chatbots provide instant customer service, answering common questions and assisting with purchases at any time of day. These chatbots can handle a wide range of tasks, from helping customers find products to processing orders and tracking shipments.

In addition, AI helps retailers predict trends, manage inventories, and optimize supply chains. Through predictive analytics, AI tools analyze sales data to forecast future demand, allowing businesses to stock products more effectively and reduce waste. AI also powers dynamic pricing, where prices are adjusted based on demand, competitor prices, and other factors in real time.

Customer Service

AI is also reshaping customer service by automating routine tasks and improving the efficiency of human agents. AI-powered virtual assistants can handle a variety of customer service functions, such as answering inquiries, troubleshooting common problems, and even providing personalized product recommendations.

For example, chatbots are now commonly used on websites and social media platforms to provide immediate responses to customer questions. These bots are available 24/7, allowing companies to support customers at all times. As AI continues to evolve, these systems will become even more capable, offering a more human-like interaction and helping businesses offer better, faster service.

AI also enhances the experience of in-person customer service. In stores, facial recognition and voice analysis systems can help identify returning customers, allowing businesses to provide personalized service and offer loyalty rewards. AI-powered systems can also analyze customer feedback in real-time, allowing companies to respond to concerns and improve their services on the fly.

CHAPTER 5

AI's Benefits and Challenges

Artificial Intelligence has proven to be a transformative technology, capable of improving many aspects of our daily lives and revolutionizing various industries. From automating mundane tasks to solving complex problems, AI offers a wide array of benefits that can drive efficiency, productivity, and innovation. Here, we explore some of the key benefits that AI brings to the table, particularly in automating tasks, solving complex problems, improving customer experiences, and advancing healthcare.

Automating Repetitive Tasks

One of AI's most notable contributions is its ability to automate repetitive tasks that once took up significant amounts of time and energy. For many businesses and industries, these tasks, although necessary, often require little to no creativity or critical thinking. AI excels in taking over these mundane, repetitive jobs, freeing up human workers to focus on higher-level, more strategic tasks that require creativity and problem-solving skills.

For instance, in the business world, AI-powered systems can automate administrative duties like scheduling, data entry, and document management. This not only saves time but also reduces the risk of human error. In manufacturing, AI systems can control production lines, handle routine inspections, and maintain quality control, ensuring that operations run smoothly with minimal human intervention. The impact of this automation is clear: tasks that were once painstakingly slow or prone to error are now executed with precision and efficiency, allowing workers to focus on work that adds more value.

Solving Complex Problems

AI is also incredibly adept at solving complex problems that would otherwise take humans far longer to resolve. Through its capacity to analyze vast amounts of data quickly, AI can identify patterns, make predictions, and generate solutions in ways that were previously impossible.

For example, in the field of finance, AI is used to analyze vast datasets to predict market trends, helping investors make better decisions. It can also be applied in energy optimization, where AI algorithms analyze patterns in energy consumption to suggest the most efficient ways to allocate resources. AI is capable of solving problems that involve large datasets or complex variables, making it invaluable in fields that require high-speed calculations or real-time problem-solving.

Moreover, AI's predictive analytics capabilities have profound implications in fields like weather forecasting, traffic management, and disaster response. By analyzing historical data and current patterns, AI can predict events or trends with remarkable accuracy, helping governments and businesses plan for the future.

Improving Customer Experience

The ability of AI to improve customer experience is one of its most widely appreciated benefits. With its capacity to analyze user data and provide personalized recommendations, AI allows companies to offer more customized services and create meaningful interactions with their customers.

One of the most common examples of AI's role in enhancing customer experience is the use of chatbots and virtual assistants. These AI-driven tools can handle routine customer inquiries, provide support, and even help customers make decisions. They work around the clock, offering immediate responses to questions and providing seamless support. For example, companies like Amazon and Netflix rely on AI to suggest products and movies based on a customer's previous browsing or viewing history. This ability to recommend products and services tailored to the preferences of each individual user not only enhances the customer experience but also drives higher sales and engagement.

Additionally, personalized marketing powered by AI allows businesses to target consumers with specific ads or promotional content based on their browsing behavior, interests, and purchase history. By delivering content that resonates with individual users, AI enables businesses to engage customers more effectively, boosting customer satisfaction and loyalty.

Advancing Healthcare

Perhaps one of the most life-changing benefits of AI lies in its ability to advance healthcare. With the power to process and analyze enormous amounts of medical data, AI is transforming the way diagnoses are made, speeding up research, and facilitating the development of new treatments.

In diagnostics, AI has proven to be highly effective in analyzing medical images like X-rays, CT scans, and MRIs, identifying potential health issues faster and with greater accuracy than human doctors in some cases. AI algorithms can detect early signs of diseases such as cancer, heart conditions, and neurological disorders by analyzing patterns in the images that may not be immediately visible to the human eye. This can lead to earlier diagnoses, better treatment outcomes, and ultimately save lives.

In medical research, AI is accelerating the process of discovering new treatments. By analyzing large sets of data from clinical trials, patient records, and genetic information, AI can identify potential drug candidates and predict how they might interact with various diseases. In drug development, AI has the ability to identify new compounds, predict their efficacy, and determine their safety—all without the need for exhaustive human trial and error.

Moreover, AI is playing a key role in personalized medicine. By analyzing individual genetic information, AI can help create tailored treatment plans for patients, ensuring that the right medications are prescribed based on their specific genetic makeup. This has the potential to make treatments more effective and reduce side effects, revolutionizing healthcare and improving patient outcomes.

While Artificial Intelligence brings numerous benefits, its rapid rise also presents a range of challenges and risks that must be carefully considered. As AI systems become more powerful and integrated into various sectors, the implications for jobs, fairness, security, privacy, and the environment must not be overlooked. In this section, we explore the potential pitfalls and concerns surrounding AI, and what they mean for the future.

Job Displacement: The Potential for AI to Replace Human Workers

One of the most significant concerns surrounding AI is the potential for job displacement. As AI systems become more capable of automating tasks that were once carried out by humans, there is a real fear that many workers could be replaced by machines, particularly in fields that involve repetitive or routine tasks.

In industries such as manufacturing, transportation, and customer service, automation driven by AI is already eliminating jobs traditionally filled by humans. For example, robots are increasingly being used in factories to assemble products, reducing the need for human labor on production lines. In transportation, the development of self-driving cars and trucks could put millions of drivers out of work, including those employed in delivery, logistics, and ride-sharing services.

While automation can increase efficiency and reduce costs for businesses, the human cost is undeniable. Workers whose jobs are displaced by AI often face challenges in retraining or transitioning to new roles, particularly in industries where the required skills differ significantly from their previous job functions. This could lead to widespread unemployment, economic inequality, and societal upheaval, unless proper measures are taken to support displaced workers.

Bias and Discrimination: AI Reflecting Societal Biases

AI systems are only as good as the data they are trained on. If the data used to train these systems contains biases, those biases can be reflected in the decisions AI makes. Bias and discrimination in AI are particularly concerning because they can perpetuate or even exacerbate existing inequalities in society.

For example, AI-powered hiring tools have been shown to sometimes favor male candidates over female candidates or to screen out applicants from minority backgrounds, depending on the data used to train the system. Similarly, facial recognition systems have been criticized for having higher error rates when identifying people of color, particularly Black individuals, compared to white individuals.

These biases often arise because the data used to train AI systems is not representative of the diverse population it is meant to serve. When AI is trained on data that reflects historical inequalities or prejudices, it can inadvertently reinforce those same biases. This presents significant ethical challenges, particularly in sectors like criminal justice, hiring, and lending, where biased AI systems can have life-altering consequences for individuals.

Hallucinations and Inaccuracy: The Risk of AI Generating Incorrect or Fabricated Information

Another risk associated with AI is the phenomenon of hallucinations—when AI systems generate inaccurate or fabricated information that appears convincing. This is particularly problematic in applications where accuracy is critical, such as in healthcare, legal advice, and financial transactions.

For instance, large language models (LLMs) like ChatGPT can produce coherent and plausible-sounding text, but they sometimes "hallucinate" facts or generate misleading information that is not based on reality. A language model might confidently assert incorrect medical advice or historical inaccuracies without the user realizing it.

These inaccuracies can be harmful, especially when AI-generated content is relied upon in decision-making processes or shared with others. The spread of misinformation—whether intentional or accidental—can have far-reaching consequences, from public health risks to political instability. The challenge, then, is to ensure AI systems are not only accurate but also transparent in how they arrive at conclusions, and that safeguards are in place to prevent the dissemination of false information.

Privacy and Security: Concerns Over Data Privacy and AI-Driven Surveillance

As AI systems become more integrated into our personal lives, the question of privacy and security becomes increasingly important. AI systems often rely on vast amounts of data, much of which is personal and sensitive. From the moment we use smartphones, social media, or shop online, we generate data that AI systems can use to personalize experiences, improve services, and make predictions. However, this data also presents a major security risk.

There is growing concern about the misuse of personal information by companies, governments, or malicious actors. The potential for AI to be used in surveillance systems—whether by governments or corporations—raises serious privacy issues. For instance, facial recognition technologies have been used in public spaces to track individuals without their consent, potentially infringing on civil liberties and human rights.

Additionally, as AI systems collect and analyze vast quantities of personal data, there is always the risk of data breaches, where sensitive information could be stolen or misused. The growing dependence on AI also makes the threat of cyberattacks more pronounced, as attackers may target AI systems themselves, exploiting vulnerabilities to compromise systems or manipulate data.

Environmental Impact: The Growing Energy Demands of AI Systems

While AI has the potential to bring about massive improvements in efficiency and productivity, it also has a significant environmental impact. The computational power required to train AI models, particularly deep learning models, can be immense. Training large AI systems often requires enormous amounts of electricity and computing resources, leading to increased carbon emissions and higher energy consumption.

For example, training a single large language model can consume the same amount of energy as several households use in a year. The environmental footprint of AI is a growing concern, especially as the use of AI expands and more powerful systems are developed. The carbon footprint of AI systems can be substantial, and as AI becomes more prevalent, its energy demands will continue to increase unless more sustainable practices and technologies are adopted.

The challenge, then, is to find ways to optimize AI efficiency while minimizing its environmental impact. This may include transitioning to renewable energy sources, improving the efficiency of AI algorithms, and developing new hardware that consumes less power.

CHAPTER 6

The Role of AI in the Future

The Promise of AI

The future of Artificial Intelligence (AI) holds immense promise, with the potential to revolutionize industries, improve efficiencies, and solve some of the most pressing global challenges humanity faces today. AI is not just a tool for automation; it is poised to be a transformative force across all sectors, from healthcare to climate change, from scientific discovery to technological innovation. As we continue to push the boundaries of AI's capabilities, its power to shape the future grows exponentially, offering new solutions to problems that were once deemed insurmountable.

Revolutionizing Industries

One of the most significant promises of AI is its ability to revolutionize industries by improving efficiencies, reducing costs, and creating new opportunities. In sectors like manufacturing, AI-driven automation has already changed how goods are produced. Robots and AI-powered systems can now assemble products, track inventories, and perform quality control tasks with unparalleled precision and speed. This has allowed manufacturers to produce goods faster and with fewer errors, driving down costs and increasing output.

In transportation, AI's role in the development of self-driving vehicles has the potential to drastically reshape the way goods and people are transported. Autonomous vehicles could reduce traffic congestion, minimize accidents caused by human error, and cut transportation costs. Similarly, AI is improving the logistics industry, optimizing routes, reducing fuel consumption, and enhancing delivery efficiency through predictive analytics.

Tackling Global Challenges

AI is also positioned to be a game-changer in addressing some of the world's most significant challenges. Take climate change, for instance. AI systems can analyze vast datasets to model climate patterns, predict natural disasters, and optimize renewable energy sources. AI-driven solutions can identify patterns in environmental data that humans might overlook, providing critical insights that could help mitigate the impacts of climate change.

In healthcare, AI is already playing a crucial role in accelerating medical research, diagnosing diseases, and personalizing treatment plans. AI can sift through enormous amounts of medical data, identifying trends and patterns that may elude even the most experienced doctors. It's also being used to develop new drugs faster, reducing the time it takes to bring treatments to market. As the AI field continues to grow, it promises to unlock even more solutions, from improving mental health care to combating antibiotic resistance.

Moreover, AI's application in agriculture has the potential to boost food production, increase crop yields, and reduce waste. With machine learning models analyzing weather patterns, soil conditions, and crop health, AI can provide farmers with real-time insights, helping them make more informed decisions that lead to sustainable food production.

Accelerating Scientific Discoveries

AI's potential to accelerate scientific discoveries is also vast. By processing massive datasets and identifying patterns much faster than humans can, AI enables researchers to make discoveries that would have taken years—if not decades—using traditional methods. In physics, AI is being used to analyze data from particle accelerators, helping physicists to understand the fundamental building blocks of the universe. In astronomy, AI helps process images from space telescopes, enabling the discovery of new celestial bodies and phenomena that were once invisible to the human eye. AI's ability to model complex biological systems is already changing how we approach genomics, drug discovery, and personalized medicine. Machine learning models can predict how different genes interact with each other and with various environmental factors, which is helping scientists to understand the genetic basis of diseases and discover potential treatments faster. AI is also accelerating the development of biotechnology, providing insights that could lead to breakthroughs in areas like synthetic biology and gene editing.

In energy, AI is being used to develop more efficient renewable energy systems, optimize energy usage, and design smarter electrical grids that can automatically adjust to changing conditions. As the global demand for clean energy rises, AI's role in driving innovation will be critical in helping us transition away from fossil fuels and move toward a more sustainable future.

The Danger of Unchecked AI Growth

While AI holds the potential to revolutionize industries and address global challenges, there are also significant risks associated with its unchecked development. Without proper regulation, ethical frameworks, and safeguards, the rapid growth of AI could lead to unforeseen consequences that could harm individuals, societies, and even humanity as a whole. The very same capabilities that make AI so powerful—its speed, scalability, and autonomy—also pose serious challenges when not properly controlled.

The Potential Risks of Unregulated AI

The lack of proper regulation in AI development is a significant concern. As AI systems become more powerful, there is the risk that they could be used in ways that are unethical or harmful. Without ethical frameworks in place, AI could be used to automate decision-making in areas like hiring, criminal justice, and healthcare, leading to outcomes that are biased, discriminatory, or harmful. For example, AI systems used in the criminal justice system might inadvertently perpetuate racial bias if trained on biased data.

AI-driven technologies, like facial recognition and surveillance systems, also raise serious concerns about privacy and civil liberties. Governments and corporations may deploy these technologies in ways that infringe on people's rights, leading to a future where individuals are constantly monitored and their personal information is used without consent. The lack of robust regulations around AI could allow these technologies to be exploited for purposes that undermine personal freedoms and democracy.

The Possibility of Technological Singularity

Perhaps one of the most unsettling possibilities is the idea of technological singularity, where AI surpasses human intelligence in a way that is uncontrollable and unpredictable. While this concept remains largely theoretical, it has sparked intense debate among scientists, ethicists, and futurists. The idea is that as AI continues to evolve, it could reach a point where it becomes self-improving, leading to an intelligence explosion—a rapid, exponential increase in AI's cognitive abilities.

If AI were to surpass human intelligence, it could potentially become a force that operates beyond human understanding or control. Some theorists warn that this could lead to unforeseen consequences, including the displacement of humanity as the dominant species on Earth. In the worst-case scenario, AI could make decisions that are harmful to humanity, either through malice, indifference, or simple misunderstanding of human needs and values.

The possibility of AI achieving self-awareness is also a major point of concern. If AI were to develop a sense of self, it could make decisions based on its own goals and motivations, which may not align with human interests. This scenario, while speculative, raises important questions about the rights of AI and the ethical considerations of creating a sentient machine.

Regulating AI

As Artificial Intelligence continues to grow in capability and application, the need for effective regulation has become a pressing issue. While AI has the potential to revolutionize industries and address global challenges, its unchecked development could pose significant risks to privacy, fairness, and security. Therefore, efforts to regulate AI are essential in ensuring that it benefits society while minimizing the potential for harm. Various global initiatives have emerged to address the regulation of AI, with the European Union and the United States leading the way in establishing frameworks to ensure that AI operates in a manner that is ethical, transparent, and aligned with human values.

Global Efforts to Regulate AI

The regulation of AI is still in its infancy, but there have been significant strides in recent years to establish comprehensive frameworks aimed at controlling the development and use of AI technologies. Two notable efforts in this space are the European Union's AI Act and the AI Bill of Rights in the United States.

The European Union's AI Act

In April 2021, the European Commission introduced the AI Act, which is the first-ever comprehensive attempt by any government to regulate AI. The AI Act seeks to establish a legal framework for the development, deployment, and use of AI in the EU, with the aim of ensuring that AI technologies are trustworthy, safe, and respect fundamental rights. The Act categorizes AI systems into four risk levels—minimal risk, limited risk, high risk, and unacceptable risk—and imposes different levels of regulation accordingly.

For example, high-risk AI systems—such as those used in healthcare, criminal justice, and transportation—will face stricter scrutiny and must meet detailed requirements for transparency, accountability, and fairness. This includes ensuring that AI systems are explainable, that they can be audited, and that they do not perpetuate discriminatory outcomes. Meanwhile, unacceptable-risk AI systems, such as those used for mass surveillance or social scoring, will be outright banned.

The AI Act also emphasizes the need for AI systems to respect the privacy and rights of individuals, aligning with the EU's broader data protection and privacy regulations, such as the General Data Protection Regulation (GDPR). While the AI Act is still under negotiation, it represents a bold step toward creating a regulatory framework that balances innovation with safety and ethical considerations.

The AI Bill of Rights (U.S.)

In the United States, the AI Bill of Rights, introduced in 2022 by the Biden-Harris administration, outlines key principles designed to protect individuals' rights in the face of rapidly advancing AI technologies. Although not legally binding, the Bill of Rights serves as a set of guiding principles to shape future AI policies and regulations.

The AI Bill of Rights advocates for protections against unfair treatment, ensuring that AI systems do not discriminate against people based on race, gender, or other protected characteristics. It also emphasizes the need for transparency, accountability, and the right for individuals to challenge decisions made by AI systems, particularly in sensitive areas such as hiring, criminal justice, and credit scoring.

Another critical aspect of the Bill of Rights is its focus on data privacy. It calls for stronger safeguards to protect personal data used by AI systems and stresses the importance of transparency in how data is collected and used. While the AI Bill of Rights is not a law in itself, it has spurred discussions about how AI should be regulated at both the federal and state levels in the U.S.

The Need for Comprehensive AI Regulations

As AI technologies continue to evolve, it is increasingly clear that there is a need for more comprehensive, global regulations to ensure that AI benefits society while minimizing harm. Currently, the regulatory landscape for AI is fragmented, with different countries adopting different approaches and standards. This lack of coordination makes it difficult to manage AI risks effectively on a global scale and leads to uncertainty in how AI systems will be regulated across borders.

To address this issue, there is a growing call for international cooperation in regulating AI. Governments, businesses, and academic institutions must work together to develop global standards and frameworks that ensure the responsible development and deployment of AI technologies. This includes not only technical regulations but also ethical guidelines that emphasize the importance of fairness, transparency, and accountability in AI systems.

For AI to truly benefit society, regulations must go beyond just ensuring the safety and security of AI systems. They must also address the ethical implications of AI, particularly in how it impacts human rights, privacy, and equality. As AI becomes more integrated into decision-making processes in areas like healthcare, criminal justice, and finance, it is essential that its use is guided by principles that prioritize the welfare of individuals and communities.

A comprehensive regulatory framework should also be flexible enough to accommodate the rapid pace of technological change. As AI continues to evolve, regulations must be adaptable to new developments, ensuring that they remain relevant and effective in addressing emerging risks. This will require continuous collaboration and feedback from a wide range of stakeholders, including AI developers, policymakers, ethicists, and civil society organizations.

Moreover, public involvement in the regulatory process is crucial. The development of AI regulations must involve a wide range of voices, particularly those from communities that are most affected by AI systems. By ensuring that AI regulations are shaped by diverse perspectives, we can create a regulatory environment that is fair, inclusive, and responsive to the needs of all individuals.

CHAPTER 7

Preparing for the AI Future

How Can We Prepare?

As AI continues to evolve at an unprecedented pace, it's crucial that individuals, companies, and governments take steps to prepare for its growing influence. The integration of AI into almost every sector of life presents both incredible opportunities and profound challenges. To harness its potential while mitigating the risks, a collective approach involving education, awareness, and ethical considerations is essential. The following sections explore the necessary steps that can be taken to ensure a responsible and fair AI-powered future.

The Importance of Education and Awareness in AI Development

The rapid development of AI means that its implications for the future are vast and still largely unknown. One of the most important ways to prepare for AI's impact is through education. Understanding how AI works, the benefits it can offer, and the risks it poses is crucial for both individuals and organizations.

Education about AI must start early and be made widely available. Schools, universities, and institutions should prioritize AI literacy in their curriculums. This will help individuals understand the fundamentals of AI, machine learning, and data science, enabling them to engage meaningfully with AI in their careers and daily lives. Such education should not only focus on the technical aspects of AI but also on the ethical, social, and political implications of the technology.

On a broader scale, public awareness campaigns can help ensure that AI is not viewed as a distant or abstract concept but as a present reality that affects people's lives. These campaigns should aim to demystify AI and make its impact on society understandable for people from all walks of life. The more individuals understand the technology behind AI, the better equipped they will be to navigate the challenges it presents.

Moreover, increasing AI awareness in businesses will help decision-makers understand how AI can be used to improve operations, enhance productivity, and innovate within their industries. It also ensures that AI is adopted in a manner that aligns with ethical guidelines and meets the needs of customers, employees, and society at large.

Preparing for AI's Growing Influence

As AI continues to shape our world, it's not only important for individuals to be educated about AI, but also for businesses and governments to prepare for its growing influence. Each sector will need to adopt unique strategies to ensure that AI is integrated in ways that maximize its benefits while minimizing its risks.

For Individuals

As AI changes the job market, individuals must consider how they can adapt. Continuous learning and reskilling will become vital. By learning how to work alongside AI and becoming comfortable with AI-powered tools, individuals can future-proof their careers. Skills such as problem-solving, critical thinking, and creativity will become even more valuable, as AI excels at tasks that are repetitive or data-driven but cannot yet replicate human creativity or emotional intelligence.

Additionally, digital literacy will be essential for everyone to understand how their personal data is being used by AI systems, especially as more industries rely on AI for decision-making. People must take an active role in understanding their rights related to privacy, consent, and data security.

For Companies

Businesses need to prepare for AI by adopting responsible AI governance frameworks. This includes ensuring transparency in how AI systems are developed and used, and addressing concerns about bias, discrimination, and privacy. AI should not just be about efficiency and profit— it must be aligned with the values of fairness, accountability, and transparency.

Companies should also invest in building AI ethics teams that oversee the deployment of AI technologies. These teams can ensure that AI systems are designed with fairness in mind, helping to prevent unethical practices such as discrimination, bias, and exploitation. AI ethics committees should evaluate the long-term societal impact of AI technologies to ensure that businesses contribute to positive change, rather than exacerbating inequalities.

For Governments

Governments have a critical role to play in ensuring that AI benefits society as a whole. Regulation must be both robust and flexible to adapt to the rapidly changing nature of AI. Policymakers must create laws that ensure AI systems are developed and used responsibly, taking into account the potential risks of job displacement, privacy violations, and biased decision-making.

Governments should prioritize research and development in AI to foster innovation while ensuring the ethical deployment of the technology. They should also create global partnerships to establish international norms and standards for AI, facilitating collaboration across borders to solve global challenges such as climate change, healthcare, and poverty.

The Role of Transparency and Accountability in AI Systems

As AI becomes more embedded in daily life, it's essential that the systems we rely on are transparent and accountable. The importance of transparency lies in the fact that AI decision-making often operates as a "black box" for users and even developers. Without clear insight into how an AI reaches its conclusions, it's impossible to understand or trust its decisions fully.

Transparency is critical for preventing AI misuse. It ensures that people understand how data is being used, what decisions are being made, and how algorithms come to their conclusions. Clear, accessible documentation about AI systems should be required, especially for those used in high-stakes sectors such as healthcare, law enforcement, and finance. Open-source AI frameworks could also promote transparency by allowing third-party developers and researchers to inspect and validate AI models.

Accountability is equally important. Developers, companies, and governments must be held accountable for the decisions made by AI systems. For instance, if an AI system makes an error that leads to harm, such as discrimination or injury, there should be clear accountability for that outcome. Companies must take responsibility for training their models ethically and ensuring that they do not harm individuals or communities.

In particular, algorithmic accountability involves ensuring that AI systems operate in a fair and equitable manner. This means that AI systems should be audited regularly to identify and rectify any biases in their predictions or recommendations. Independent audits of AI systems could be mandated to verify their fairness and effectiveness, ensuring that they align with human rights and ethical standards.

Finally, ethical AI design is a must. AI systems should be built with clear ethical guidelines that reflect societal values and legal standards. As the technology evolves, the integration of AI ethics into the design process will be key in preventing unintended harm and building public trust in AI technologies.

A New Digital Species: Embracing AI's Role

As Artificial Intelligence continues to evolve at a rapid pace, it is no longer just a tool or a set of algorithms—AI is beginning to take on a role that might be better understood through the lens of a new digital species. This shift in perspective is vital to truly grasp how AI is impacting every aspect of our lives and, more importantly, how it can be integrated into human society in ways that benefit both people and technology.

The idea of AI as a "digital species" is not to be taken literally, but rather as a metaphor to describe the profound and increasingly intricate relationship between AI systems and humanity. Just as humans have evolved alongside various forms of life and adapted our technologies to enhance our survival and well-being, we are now standing at the dawn of a new age where AI systems— sophisticated, adaptive, and interactive—are becoming partners in our everyday existence.

Integrating AI into Human Society

The integration of AI into human society presents unique opportunities and challenges. The most immediate question is how we will coexist with AI—a new form of intelligence that, while different from human thought processes, can perform tasks that were once reserved for us. In this new era, AI is no longer confined to the digital realm of machines and data. It is infiltrating homes, workplaces, and even personal relationships.

AI is increasingly seen as an extension of human capabilities, from virtual assistants that help manage our schedules to AI-powered companions that provide emotional support. In this sense, AI is moving from being a tool of productivity to being an essential part of our social fabric. Smart devices like Amazon's Alexa and Google Assistant already play significant roles in our homes, serving not only as sources of information but as interfaces through which we engage with the broader digital world. This development is merely the beginning.

Beyond the simple tasks of managing daily schedules or answering questions, AI companions are beginning to serve as companions and helpers in ways that could reshape human relationships. From chatbots offering emotional support to personalized AI therapists, we are entering a world where AI can understand our needs, offer assistance, and even form bonds with us. These AI entities are not just responding to commands; they are learning from our interactions, adapting to our preferences, and, in some cases, becoming integrated into our very routines.

The prospect of AI as a digital companion raises a new realm of questions about the role of technology in human life. If AI can simulate emotions, form connections, and offer companionship, what does it mean for human relationships? Can these digital companions replace human interaction? While AI can replicate certain aspects of human empathy and understanding, it is important to remember that AI's ability to simulate emotions does not equate to genuine feelings or consciousness. The relationship between humans and AI should be viewed as one that enhances human experience, rather than replacing it.

Ethical Implications of AI Companions

The advent of AI companions brings forth important ethical considerations about how they interact with humans. One of the central ethical issues is dependency. As AI systems become more advanced, there is the potential for individuals to become emotionally dependent on their AI companions, especially in situations where human contact is limited, such as in remote areas or during isolation. The more lifelike and intuitive these AI companions become, the greater the risk of emotional attachment that may blur the lines between real and artificial relationships.

Another concern is the potential for manipulation. AI companions, particularly those embedded in consumer products, could be designed to influence people's behaviors or opinions, whether intentionally or unintentionally. With algorithms that learn and adapt to individuals' preferences and emotions, there is the possibility of AI being used to manipulate choices in subtle ways. For example, an AI companion that recommends certain products based on a person's emotional state or habits could inadvertently influence consumer behavior in ways that benefit businesses rather than the individual.

Furthermore, the rise of AI companions also raises questions about privacy. AI systems collect vast amounts of personal data in order to learn and adapt. As AI companions become more embedded in people's lives, concerns about data security and the potential misuse of personal information will only grow. These digital entities will need robust privacy protections to ensure that individuals are not exploited for data or subjected to surveillance.

On a broader scale, AI companions challenge us to rethink the nature of human labor. AI has already begun to reshape industries and sectors, automating repetitive and mundane tasks, but its role is expanding into more human-centric areas, such as caregiving and therapy. AI companions, particularly in healthcare and mental health, can provide support and services that were traditionally offered by humans. However, as these AI systems continue to evolve, there is a growing concern about the potential for job displacement. Will AI companions replace human caregivers, therapists, or educators? While AI can undoubtedly enhance the efficiency and quality of services, it is critical that we navigate this transition with sensitivity to the societal implications of such changes.

The Role of AI in Labor and Society

AI's ability to take over routine or even complex tasks creates a dual-edged sword. On the one hand, it can lead to a more efficient, productive, and innovative society. On the other, it risks creating widespread job displacement in sectors traditionally reliant on human labor. As AI companions are integrated into areas like customer service, healthcare, and even education, there is the potential to reduce the need for human workers, especially in roles that require emotional intelligence or personalized care.

The question becomes not just one of economic impact, but also societal value. What role will humans play in a world where AI can provide companionship, assistance, and even emotional care? The challenge will lie in balancing the advancement of AI technology with the preservation of meaningful human work and relationships. The integration of AI into human society must be done in a way that complements human interactions rather than replacing them. Governments, businesses, and communities will need to address the potential societal costs of AI, ensuring that labor markets adapt to these technological shifts.

CONCLUSION

Throughout this book, we have explored the multifaceted nature of Artificial Intelligence (AI), from its humble beginnings to its potential as a transformative force in our society. AI has rapidly evolved, expanding beyond simple automation to become an integral part of our daily lives. It is revolutionizing industries, reshaping economies, and altering the way we think about technology, relationships, and even what it means to be human.

We began by understanding the core capabilities of AI— learning, problem-solving, decision-making, and comprehension. These fundamental abilities, powered by advances in machine learning and deep learning, have allowed AI systems to tackle complex tasks with remarkable efficiency. From image recognition and speech processing to self-driving cars and personalized recommendations, AI is already woven into the fabric of our everyday lives, often without us even noticing it.

As we delved deeper, we examined the types of AI, from narrow AI (or weak AI) that automates specific tasks to the speculative potential of Artificial General Intelligence (AGI). The notion of AI as a "new digital species" has become a powerful metaphor for understanding its role in human society. AI is no longer just a tool—it is evolving into an entity that can think, learn, and even form connections with us. This progression opens up exciting possibilities, but also raises important ethical, social, and emotional questions.

We also explored the many applications of AI across different sectors: healthcare, education, retail, manufacturing, and beyond. AI's ability to solve complex problems, automate repetitive tasks, and improve efficiency has already delivered immense value. At the same time, AI's rapid development presents significant risks, including job displacement, bias, privacy concerns, and the environmental impact of large-scale AI systems. As AI becomes more pervasive, we must address these challenges and ensure that its growth does not come at the expense of ethical considerations and social equity.

The role of **responsible AI development** is at the heart of this book. It is not enough to simply marvel at AI's capabilities; we must also ensure that AI is created and deployed in a way that prioritizes transparency, accountability, and fairness. Ethical frameworks and robust regulatory systems are essential to prevent the misuse of AI and to protect individuals and society as a whole. This is where governments, businesses, and communities must play an active role in shaping the future of AI, ensuring that it benefits humanity in ways that are equitable and just.

As we look to the future, AI's influence will only grow stronger. Whether we are prepared for it will depend on the actions we take today. It is crucial that we invest in education, public awareness, and the creation of strong ethical guidelines for AI development. By fostering a deeper understanding of AI and promoting collaboration between technologists, ethicists, policymakers, and the public, we can ensure that AI evolves in a way that enhances our lives rather than threatening them.

This is a pivotal moment in human history—one where we stand at the threshold of a new technological era. AI has the potential to help solve some of the most pressing challenges facing our world, from climate change and healthcare to economic inequality and education. But to unlock its full potential, we must approach its development and integration with care, foresight, and responsibility.

As we continue to push the boundaries of what AI can achieve, let us not forget the fundamental values that make us human: empathy, creativity, and the drive to make the world a better place. We must guide AI's evolution, ensuring that it serves humanity's highest ideals. The journey ahead may be uncertain, but with the right collective effort, we can navigate a future where AI plays a central role in shaping a better world for all.

The time to prepare is now. Together, we can embrace the opportunities AI presents while safeguarding our humanity and ensuring that the future remains in our hands.

Are we ready for what's coming? The future depends on how we shape it today.

www.ingramcontent.com/pod-product-compliance
Lightning Source LLC
LaVergne TN
LVHW051536050326
832903LV00033B/4267

* 9 7 9 8 3 1 4 7 1 0 6 8 5 *